Meet the Saints
Family Storybook

Melody Wilson Shobe
and
Lindsay Hardin Freeman

Forward Movement · Cincinnati, Ohio

ISBN 978-0-88028-421-9

Forward Movement
412 Sycamore Street
Cincinnati, Ohio USA 45202

The creation of the *Living Discipleship* curriculum has been supported by
a generous grant from The Episcopal Church's Constable Fund.

Illustrations by Daniel Dufford

Forward
Movement
www.forwardmovement.org

Table of Contents

Introduction

Welcome to *Meet the Saints: Family Storybook!* If you are a parent or teacher reading this, you are blessed to have God's young ones in your care. And if you are a kid reading this, you are blessed because Jesus holds children very close to his heart.

In this storybook, you will meet some of the great **saints** of our church (You can even color some of them!). These saints are not always what you would expect. Some of them were priests, but some were poets. Some were monks, and some were musicians. Some were old and some were young. Some lived in Jesus' time, while others lived only a few years ago.

All of them were tough, brave—and most of all, **faithful**. They loved God with all their hearts and souls and minds and strength. And they loved Jesus so much they were willing to follow him wherever he led, even if it wasn't safe.

The lives of the saints were not always easy. They had hard times, were hurt or sad, and even died. Yet they have much to **teach** us, for we also live in hard and difficult times. Sometimes we feel hurt or sad or scared. Sometimes people we love get sick or even die.

And it is in those times, most of all, that we need our faith. It is in those times that Jesus holds us more tightly than ever. The lessons of our spiritual ancestors—the saints of God —help us to know how to be brave, how to survive, how to help others, and how to always call on God.

The truth is, the saints of God aren't just people who lived long ago and far away. The saints of God are just folks like you and me. They surround us, a great cloud of witnesses, the communion of saints. As we learn about them, we learn about the life of faith. As we grow close to them, we grow close to Jesus, who **loves** each of us, calls us by name, and makes us his saints.

So let's get ready to **celebrate** the saints. Have fun and hold on to your hats, because the journey of following Jesus is always a wild ride.

Blessings,

Melody Wilson Shobe &
Lindsay Hardin Freeman

Meet the Saints

Almighty God, you have surrounded us with a great cloud of witnesses: Grant that we, encouraged by the good example of your servants may persevere in running the race that is set before us, until at last we may with them attain to your eternal joy; through Jesus Christ, the pioneer and perfecter of our faith, who lives and reigns with you and the Holy Spirit, one God, for ever and ever. **Amen.** (*The Book of Common Prayer*, p. 250)

Tell me a story

Lesbia Scott loved her children very much, and she loved music very much. When her children were small, they would ask her to write songs for them. "Write us a song about the birds singing," one child would ask. And she did. "Sing to us about our picnic!" another child would beg. And she did.

Lesbia Scott also loved God very much. So, many of the songs that she wrote were hymns: songs of praise to God, songs about love and faith and hope. Lesbia wanted her children, and children everywhere, to learn about God, and she knew that one of the best ways to learn about something is to sing about it!

One day, Lesbia decide to write a song for her children about saints. She wanted them to learn about and remember what saints are like, how they live, and where they can be found. So she sat down with her pen.

"What are saints like?" Lesbia wondered. And as she read the Bible and studied the lives of the saints in history, she learned: Saints are patient, and brave, and true. They know Jesus and love Jesus. But saints aren't superheroes. They are folks like us, people who are doctors, or shepherds, or soldiers, or moms. They don't have special powers. They do amazing things, not because they are powerful, but because God is powerful, and it is God working through them who does the amazing things. Saints aren't perfect. They sometimes stumble and fall; they sometimes mess up. But even when they fail, they return to God, and try once again to follow Jesus, their Lord.

"How do saints live?" Lesbia wondered. And as she prayed the prayers in *The Book of Common Prayer* and observed the feast days of the saints, she realized: Saints live all sorts of different lives. Some are teachers, and some are students. Some are princes, and some are poor. Some live long lives, and some die young. Some are boys, and some are girls. But all saints, no matter where they come from or who they are, try to do the right thing, even when it's hard, because they want to follow Jesus no matter what.

"Where can saints be found?" Lesbia wondered. As she looked at the witness of history and tradition and opened her eyes to the world around her, she discovered: Saints are in all places and all times. Some lived a long time ago, and many live still today. Sometimes saints spend their times in churches, and sometimes they spend their time at the mall or at school or in the park. Sometimes saints are the people who you would least expect, and they are found in the last place you would think to look.

Lesbia thought about all these things, and as she thought, a song began to come together in her mind. It was a song that would teach her children, and teach thousands of children in ages to come, about what it means to be a saint. Here's some of what she wrote:

> I sing a song of the saints of God, Patient and brave and true, Who toiled and fought and lived and died
> For the Lord they loved and knew. And one was a doctor, and one was a queen, And one was a shepherdess
> on the green; They were all of them saints of God, and I mean, God helping, to be one too.
> (The Hymnal 1982, #293)

Let's talk

The songs that we learn as children shape us in special ways. What are some of your favorite songs you learned when you were little? What did they teach you?

Who are some of the saints that you know about? What do you remember about them?

Abraham, Isaac, & Jacob

Almighty God, you have surrounded us with a great cloud of witnesses: Grant that we, encouraged by the good example of your servants **Abraham, Isaac, and Jacob**, may persevere in running the race that is set before us, until at last we may with them attain to your eternal joy; through Jesus Christ, the pioneer and perfecter of our faith, who lives and reigns with you and the Holy Spirit, one God, for ever and ever. **Amen.** (*The Book of Common Prayer*, p. 250)

Tell me a story

Thousands of years ago, in the faraway land of Haran,* there lived a man named Abraham and his wife Sarah. All of their friends had children, and many became grandparents and great-grandparents. But Sarah and Abraham were childless.

One night, when Abraham was outside looking up into the beautiful night sky, God spoke to him. "Abraham," said God. "I will make for you a great nation. But you must leave home. Go to a place that I will show you, a place that will be brimming with wonderful things to eat and see. You will have more descendants than there are stars in the sky."

Hmmm, thought Abraham. I'm already an old man. How can this be?

Abraham went home and told Sarah what God had said, and they did what God told them to do: they left home.

Back then there were no cell phones, computers, cars, planes, or hotels. Abraham and Sarah struck out into true wilderness, much of it harsh desert: cold by night and boiling hot by day. From time to time, they set up camp, accompanied by their servants, some family members, and their sheep. It was a hard and rugged journey.

As year after year went by, and Sarah did not become pregnant, they studied the night sky wondering just what God had meant: "You will have as many descendants as there are stars in the sky."

Then, one day, three men (angels in disguise) seemed to materialize right out of the desert sand. Abraham invited them to share a meal. And, as they ate, one burst out with extraordinary news. "By this time next year, Sarah will have a son!"

Immediately there was the sound of laugher. Sarah, who was overseeing meal preparations, heard the man's prediction and burst out laughing from behind the tent wall.

"How can this be at my age? Is it even possible? Abraham is one hundred years old, and I am ninety!"

A year later, Isaac—whose name means "to laugh"—was born. Isaac grew up and married Rebekah, and they were the parents of twin boys: Esau and Jacob (who later in life had his name changed to Israel by God).

Promises from God are always kept. Today, there are indeed as many descendants of Abraham as there are stars in the sky—and if you listen very hard, you still might hear Sarah's joyful laughter.

*Haran is in modern-day Turkey.

Let's talk

From what part of the world did your ancestors come? What do you remember hearing about your ancestors? What hardships might they have known?

Have you ever moved or gone on a vacation? What do you need to take with you when you move or go on a vacation? What important things might God want us to pack on our journey? How does one pack things like faith and joy and courage?

Blessed Virgin Mary

O God, you have taken to yourself the blessed **Virgin Mary**, mother of your incarnate Son: Grant that we, who have been redeemed by his blood, may share with her the glory of your eternal kingdom; through Jesus Christ our Lord, who lives and reigns with you, in the unity of the Holy Spirit, one God, now and for ever. **Amen.** (*The Book of Common Prayer*, p. 243)

Tell me a story

Mary's feet flew over the rough ground, scrambling up the hilly path toward the home of her cousin, Elizabeth. Clutching her small cloth bag to her chest, the teenage girl furiously blinked back tears, longing to fall into the older woman's arms.

Despite the difference in their ages, Mary knew that she could tell Elizabeth anything. The old woman was like a mother bear: fierce and loving, protective and daring. Perhaps because she'd never had children of her own, Elizabeth cherished Mary as a beloved daughter, one who was always welcome in the tiny house she shared with her husband Zechariah.

At that moment, Mary badly needed some comforting arms. Only hours earlier, she'd been home, alone, enjoying the solitude—an unusual moment in her large family. And in had swooped an angel, surrounded by brilliant rainbow columns of light, shimmering and weaving around his tall frame. She knew at once it was the angel Gabriel from scripture.

For once, Mary was speechless. And words rarely failed this bright and well-spoken girl. "Hail, O favored one, the Lord is with you!" announced Gabriel. What? An angel is here to see ME? The Lord is with me?

"Do not be afraid, Mary." Too late. She was afraid. "You will become pregnant, and bear a son. He will do great things and his kingdom will never end!" She knew that the angel meant now. Not years down the road, but now. "How can this be? I'm not married yet, and I've never known a man."

"The Holy Spirit will come over you. And the child will be called holy and will be the Son of God. And your cousin Elizabeth, who thought she could never have a child, has also conceived. Nothing is impossible with God!" Gabriel waited. And Mary knew that somehow an answer was required. She could say yes or no. It was up to her. Her voice rang out: "Let it be to me according to your word."

Shaking her head at what seemed an unbelievable scenario, Mary finally reached Elizabeth's house, hot and out of breath. But before she could even knock, the door flew open. Into Elizabeth's arms she fell. "Blessed are you!" Elizabeth said. "The baby in my womb is jumping for joy!"

Within minutes, Mary's tears of worry turned to tears of joy. Words tumbled forth from Mary as she praised God, in a song that today we call the *Magnificat*.

In nine short months, Jesus was born to his loving and protective parents, Mary and Joseph. Elizabeth and Zechariah's son, who was born three months after this meeting, grew up to be a wild and holy man: John the Baptist. As he had done in his mother's womb, he shared his love for Jesus without holding back.

With God, all kinds of things can happen, good things that we might not expect. And even though we may be afraid sometimes, God's love always surrounds us, much like that bright and shiny light that surrounded Gabriel. Look for it—and look for ways in which God might surprise and delight you.

Let's talk

Sometimes the stories in the Bible seem to concentrate on grownups. Yet, as is true with Mary's story, it is clear that God calls on young people to do amazing things. What might that mean for you?

Elizabeth was a good friend to Mary, helping her to remember that God was always with her. How can you be a good friend to others? Who is someone that you think God might want you to comfort or encourage? What can you do this week for that person?

We don't always see angels, yet God often communicates with us in ways that we don't always understand. What are some ways in which God might be communicating with you?

Mary Magdalene

Almighty God, whose blessed Son restored **Mary Magdalene** to health of body and of mind, and called her to be a witness of his resurrection: Mercifully grant that by your grace we may be healed from all our infirmities and know you in the power of his unending life; who with you and the Holy Spirit lives and reigns, one God, now and for ever. **Amen.** (*The Book of Common Prayer*, p. 242)

Tell me a story

It was the worst of days, and it was the best of days. The worst part came first.

Mary Magdalene's best friend, Jesus, had been killed just two days before. He had died on the cross. She had loved Jesus. And he had loved her deeply in return. She had been lonely and troubled and ill, and he healed her. He introduced Mary Magdalene to his friends, and they became her new family. Best of all, he helped her to know and love God.

Mary Magdalene knew deep inside that being a friend meant being there in bad times as well as good. Unlike many of Jesus' other friends, she had stood at the cross to give him strength. And she knew that sometimes part of loving someone who has died meant saying goodbye.

So on a cold, dark morning after the Jewish sabbath, Mary Magdalene walked slowly toward Jesus' tomb, knowing that she would not see him again—but wanting to be as close to him as she could. She knew what to expect. There would be a cave where Jesus' body lay, and a large rock blocking the cave entrance so that no one would bother Jesus' remains.

But when she reached the tomb, the rock had been moved! Her stomach twisted. Someone must have taken Jesus' body. All she wanted to do was say goodbye, and now even that was not possible.

Quickly she ran to Simon Peter's house, one of Jesus' other followers. At a lightening pace, he and another disciple named John raced to the tomb. John reached it first but stepped back to let Peter have the first look. Peering into the tomb, Peter sighed and shook his head, for the body was gone. John went in, but he too saw only the cloths in which Jesus had been wrapped.

Strong for so long, Mary Magdalene's heart yearned for Jesus. Crying, she stood alone outside the tomb—yet she would not abandon her friend and Lord. Finally, she knelt to peer into the darkness —yet the darkness was dark no longer. Two angels dressed in white met her eyes.

"Woman, why are you weeping?" What? What? "Woman, why are you weeping?" they asked.

"Because they have taken my Lord away, and I do not know where they have laid him." And then a voice came from behind her.

"Woman, why are you weeping? Whom do you seek?" Leave me alone, she thought. Can't you see that everything has gone wrong?

"Mary." That voice again! And then she knew. There Jesus stood, fully and finally recognizable. He had come back from the dead. He was alive in a new body.

"Go tell the others, Mary," said Jesus. "Tell them that I love them and that they will see me, just like you did."

And that's what she did. She was the very first person to see the risen Lord.

Let's talk

Jesus did something that no one else can do: He came back from the dead in a new body. This is called the Resurrection. How do you think you might have felt if you were Mary Magdalene at that moment?

Have you ever lost someone you loved? A friend, a grandparent or parent, a cat or a dog? Describe how you felt.

Have you ever gone to that person's grave? Have you ever buried an animal and marked its grave? How did it feel to visit that place?

Peter & Paul

Almighty God, whose blessed apostles **Peter and Paul** glorified you by their martyrdom: Grant that your Church, instructed by their teaching and example, and knit together in unity by your Spirit, may ever stand firm upon the one foundation, which is Jesus Christ our Lord; who lives and reigns with you, in the unity of the Holy Spirit, one God, now and for ever. **Amen.** (*The Book of Common Prayer*, p. 241)

Tell me a story about Peter

First, let's share a story about Peter, who fished for a living, and how he came to know and love Jesus. A strong and rugged man, Peter and his partners had spent all night out on Lake Gennesaret fishing—or rather, trying to catch fish. Sadly, their nets remained empty.

But little did he know who would need his boat that morning: Jesus. Hundreds of people had come to hear Jesus talk, and he needed a safe spot from which he could teach. Rather than get pushed into the water by the excited crowd, Jesus got in Peter's boat and asked him to take it from shore.

When Jesus finished talking, he looked over at Peter, then pointed toward the horizon. "Put out into the deep and let down your nets for a catch."

"But we fished all night and caught nothing!" said the tired Peter. Then he looked one more time at Jesus.

"At your word, I will let down the nets," Peter said.

Within minutes, the nets were so full of fish that they began breaking. Peter yelled for his partners to come help, and their boats became completely full—in fact, they almost sank under the weight.

When Peter finally reached the shore, he fell on his knees, for he had seen a miracle. The rough-and-tumble fisherman turned from the job he knew and began a new life: following Jesus. In time, he would become one of Jesus' most important disciples.

Tell me a story about Paul

Sometimes people are hard to figure out. And early on, Paul was an angry and bitter man. Known first by the name of Saul, he didn't like people who followed Jesus and did everything he could to arrest them and throw them in jail. At that time, it was against the law to be a Christian, and Saul went after Christians with a vengeance.

Armed with arrest warrants in his bag and hatred in his heart, Saul headed for Damascus, sure that he could find Christians there. As he approached the town, a blinding light from heaven flashed all about him, throwing him to the ground. In that blaze of light he heard a voice saying, "Saul, Saul, why do you persecute me?"

Paul replied: "Who are you, Master?"

"I am Jesus, the one who you are chasing down. Get up, and go into the village, where you will be told what to do."

Slowly Saul stumbled to his feet. From the outside, he looked the same, save a few bruises. But from the inside, he knew things had gone terribly wrong, for he was blind. To Damascus he went, but he did not eat nor drink.

Little did he know that a man named Ananias (An-na-Nigh-us) had also heard from God.

"Go right over to a street called Straight Avenue," Ananias heard God say. "There you will find a man named Saul, who is dreaming you will lay hands on him so that he can see again."

"Saul is a terrible person!" said Ananias. "He will arrest us and persecute us!"

"Go," said God. "Go. I've chosen Saul to be my special representative. He will do good things that you cannot even dream of."

Ananias did as God had commanded. He put his hands on Saul's eyes, and large scales dropped away from Saul's face. Not only could Saul see, but he was on fire for Jesus. For the rest of his life, he was known by the name of Paul, and he worked tirelessly to bring people to God. He founded churches throughout the region and often wrote letters to the new congregations, letters that we continue to hear in church every Sunday.

Let's talk

Both Peter and Paul turned away from their old lives and went on to new lives, following and helping Jesus. What might their decisions mean for you? How can you follow Jesus?

Both Peter and Paul used skills they already had to serve Jesus. Peter caught people for Jesus, much like he used to catch fish. Paul used the fire in his soul to turn people toward Jesus, instead of away from them. What skills and gifts do you have that you might use as you follow Jesus?

Peter & Paul

Luke the Evangelist

Almighty God, who inspired your servant **Luke** the physician to set forth in the Gospel the love and healing power of your Son: Graciously continue in your Church this love and power to heal, to the praise and glory of your Name; through Jesus Christ our Lord, who lives and reigns with you, in the unity of the Holy Spirit, one God, now and for ever. **Amen.** *(The Book of Common Prayer, pp. 244-5)*

Tell me a story

There are four gospel writers in the New Testament: Matthew, Mark, Luke, and John. They are each a little different. Luke was a friend and coworker with the apostle Paul and spent two years in jail with Paul for believing in Jesus. Luke was also a doctor, and, as you might guess, good with details.

The gospel writers sometimes have different accounts of the same event. And that is understandable. Think of four people you know: friends, parents, grandparents, siblings. If each of them were to describe Christmas or Easter, they would all tell the story differently. It's like that with the gospel writers. They all love Jesus. They all love God. They all want people to know the story. But they describe events a little differently.

Luke wrote and spoke in Greek, the language of Plato and Aristotle and Socrates. While the other gospel writers and Jesus were Jewish, Luke was not. He was called a Gentile. The word "gospel" means good news. And telling the good news story of God's love for us in Jesus is called "evangelism," so Luke was one of the world's first evangelists.

A loving and kind man, Luke had a special place in his heart for prayer and praising God. Poetry flowed from his heart, especially when recounting stories about Jesus and how people found their happiness in him. Here is an example of a story that only Luke told:

When Jesus was a baby, his parents did what all Jewish parents of firstborn boys did: They brought him to the temple in Jerusalem to dedicate him to God. In the temple was an old man named Simeon. Deep in Simeon's heart, he knew one thing: that God's son would be born and would save the world. Waiting a lifetime might have driven other people crazy. But Simeon, a patient and holy man, kept praying.

One day the Holy Spirit told him it was time: Jesus was near. Breathing deeply, he rushed to the temple— and there was Jesus, the Son of God! As was the custom, he took the baby into his arms and blessed him.

"Lord, I can now die in peace," said Simeon. "With my own eyes I have seen the salvation of the world, a light for all, and glory for the people of Israel."

Simeon died a happy old man. He knew that God would keep his promise, and God did. Such a story made Luke happy as well. Perhaps, at the end of his life, he felt a little like Simeon did: his eyes had known the glory of God, and he had done all he could to tell the world about Jesus.

As Luke would say, "Praise be to God!"

Let's talk

Luke was an evangelist, someone who told other people the good news of God. What are some ways that you can share the good news of God with others?

Luke was a great storyteller. What are your favorite stories to tell? How did you learn to tell those stories? What is your favorite part of Jesus' story?

Perpetua and Her Companions

O God the King of saints, you strengthened your servants **Perpetua** and Felicitas and their companions to make a good confession, staunchly resisting, for the cause of Christ, the claims of human affection, and encouraging one another in their time of trial: Grant that we who cherish their blessed memory may share their pure and steadfast victory; and win with them the palm of victory; through Jesus Christ our Lord, who lives and reigns with you and the Holy Spirit, one God, for ever and ever. **Amen.** (*Lesser Feasts and Fasts*, p. 189)

Tell me a story

There is an old belief that children cannot bear hard stories. Yet you may have experienced times when life was hard or unfair. Sometimes people we love go away, or even die. Sometimes the actions of friends, parents, or teachers hurt us. Sometimes the world itself seems scary. That's why it's a good thing to learn the stories of saints.

Saints knew that bad things happen, but they also knew that God loved them. And God loves us too, more than we can ever know. Even in the darkest of nights, God is always with us, always on our side, always our protector, our friend, our companion.

Few saints knew that truth better than Perpetua (per-PEH-tshoo-uh), who lived about 150 years after Jesus and Mary Magdalene. Born into a wealthy family in North Africa in about 181 CE, she didn't know much about Jesus or God at first. The more she learned as she prepared to be baptized, however, the more she fell in love. She decided that nothing was more important than Jesus, and she decided to put him first in everything that she did.

In those days, people did not have the freedom to believe in God that most of us have today. Early Christians, in fact, often faced life and death decisions. If they did not swear their allegiance to the Roman Empire, sadly, they were often killed. Sometimes soldiers put them to death. Other times they were eaten by hungry lions in public arenas.

Despite this threat, Perpetua and her servants, Felicitas (fuh-LEE-see-tas) and Revocatus (re-VOH-ki-tuhs), stayed firm. Jesus was their friend, and they would be his. Even after they were jailed for their faith, they did not waver or change their minds. One of the hardest things for Perpetua was that this meant she had to be separated from her young son. No mother wants to leave her child, but Perpetua decided that the best way to be a mother was to be true and honest and strong about who she was, first and foremost: a Christian, even though it put her life at risk.

Have you ever had a dream that you remembered when you woke up? Perpetua had vivid dreams while in prison that helped her to be brave. Once she dreamed she was climbing a ladder to heaven, and another time she saw herself battling the devil—and winning. Even though her father asked her several times to swear that she was loyal to the emperor over God, she would not do it.

Finally, Perpetua was killed because of her faith. To the very end, she kept Jesus at the center of her thoughts and actions. Other Christians were forced to watch her final moments. Her final words to them remain an inspiration to us today: "Stand fast in the faith and love one another!" she said. "And do not let what we suffer be a stumbling block to you."

Let's talk

Church congregations can often serve as big families. Are there any people in your church family who feel like extra parents or grandparents?

Have you, like Perpetua, ever had a dream that helped you stay brave? Describe it or draw it.

It is hard to lose a parent like Perpetua's son did, when his mother was killed. Although it doesn't happen very often, sometimes parents die or move away from their children. Do you know someone who has lost a parent? Or have you? How can God help us when that happens?

John Chrysostom

O God, you gave your servant **John Chrysostom** grace eloquently to proclaim your righteousness in the great congregation, and fearlessly to bear reproach for the honor of your Name: Mercifully grant to all bishops and pastors such excellence in preaching, and faithfulness in ministering your Word, that your people may be partakers with them of the glory that shall be revealed; through Jesus Christ our Lord, who lives and reigns with you and the Holy Spirit, one God, for ever and ever. **Amen.** (*Lesser Feasts and Fasts*, p. 151)

Tell me a story

Saints never lived easy lives, for it takes great inner and outer strength to follow Jesus. And although saints can be people of all ages, it takes much vigor to stand up for God for a lifetime.

John Chrysostom (Kriz-zos-tum) was one of those who did. Strong as steel and fiery as the Fourth of July, he was such a good preacher that his name, Chrysostom, means "golden-mouthed." Early Christians flocked to hear his sermons. Legend has it that listeners became easy targets for pickpockets because they became completely transfixed on John's preaching, and they weren't paying attention to anything else.

What made his preaching so good? Three things: he loved Jesus, he told the truth, and he particularly loved poor and ordinary people. In his day, preachers would often speak from the altar, located far away from the listeners. But not John. He was the first to speak from a moveable stand called a pulpit, so that he could be as close as possible to the congregation. God's love rolled out of him like waves on a beach: never-ending and with great power.

Churches and cathedrals are often quiet places. Yet when John preached, applause was so loud that it would rise to the ceiling, bouncing off the stone walls. Such affirmation might have gone to some people's heads. But not John. He remained a humble servant of God, finding just the right words from deep in his prayer-filled soul.

Living in a time of great political upheaval, John's influence was felt far and wide among the people of Constantinople. On the side of the common man and woman, John often criticized those in power, including friends and fellow church leaders, when he felt they weren't living up to the high standards God wanted. And that is what eventually got him in trouble. Empress Eudoxia (U-dox-ee-a), the highest-ranking woman in eastern Greece, started out as his friend, but John made no secret of the fact that he believed she was living a lavish lifestyle. When she had a silver statue of herself built on the cathedral steps, John publicly criticized her.

Angry beyond words at the fiery preacher, Eudoxia argued for the leaders of the church to throw him out of power, and eventually, she succeeded. John was taken on a forced march through the deserts of eastern Turkey, and there he died.

When Pope Innocent found out about the way John had been treated, he insisted that church leaders apologize. In every century since then, John's words and brilliant preaching style have risen like a beautiful kite in the sky: dancing near the heavens, never to be forgotten, one of a kind.

Let's talk

What was your favorite part about the sermon this week (or last week)? What do you think makes a sermon good? What are some things that you could do to help you listen to the sermon carefully?

Below is a prayer written by John Chrysostom. Read it aloud, or listen to someone else read it. What does it say? What might it say about the man who wrote it?

Almighty God, you have given us grace at this time with one accord to make our common supplication to you; and you have promised through your well-beloved Son that when two or three are gathered together in his Name you will be in the midst of them: Fulfill now, O Lord, our desires and petitions as may be best for us; granting us in this world knowledge of your truth, and in the age to come life everlasting. *Amen.*

Patrick & Brigid

Almighty God, in your providence you chose your servant **Patrick** to be the apostle of the Irish people, to bring those who were wandering in darkness and error to the true light and knowledge of you: Grant us so to walk in that light that we may come at last to the light of everlasting life; through Jesus Christ our Lord, who lives and reigns with you and the Holy Spirit, one God, for ever and ever. **Amen.** *(Lesser Feasts and Fasts,* p. 197)

Everliving God, we rejoice today in the fellowship of your blessed servant **Brigid,** and we give you thanks for her life of devoted service. Inspire us with life and light, and give us perseverance to serve you all our days; through Jesus Christ our Lord, who with you and the Holy Spirit lives and reigns, one God, for ever and ever. **Amen.** *(Lesser Feasts and Fasts,* p. 155)

Tell me a story about Patrick

Trying in vain to find a comfortable spot, Patrick leaned back against the sharp rocks for what seemed the thousandth time. Cold and jagged, they reminded him of how much he missed his bed at home and how long it had been since he'd laid down without a care. He thought of how he'd come to Ireland six years before: kidnapped, bound, and carried away from England's shores by pirates. In slavery since then, he had tended sheep on the lonely mountain slopes of northwest Ireland.

As lonely as his hours were, Patrick knew the presence of God: strong, bright, comforting. Within the span of a single day, he would say as many as two hundred prayers. Picture Patrick: strong, lanky, rugged, and in continual conversation with Jesus, the true Shepherd.

One night a vision—as lofty as the mountains and as bright as the stars—convinced Patrick to run away from his master in search of freedom and home. Covering some two hundred miles by foot, he arrived at a port where a ship was about to set sail. Penniless, he convinced the crew to allow him safe passage.

Eventually Patrick found his way back to Britain and into the joyful arms of friends and family. But it wasn't enough. Years of walking with God on those Irish hills had changed him into a mountain of a man: immovable in his faith and dedicated to guiding others to Christ. He studied theology and the Bible and was ordained a priest in the Church.

And then came the shocking news, straight from Patrick's heart: he would move back to Ireland, the place where he had toiled so long in slavery. He knew the language and the customs, and he longed to share the news of Christ. While Christianity had touched Ireland's shores hundreds of years previously, the majority of the Irish did not know Jesus in their hearts like Patrick did.

Full of fire, Patrick returned to Ireland. Over the years, he baptized thousands, became a bishop, ordained priests to start new communities of faith, and fought off evil whenever it crossed his path. Rough and rugged and protective of God's people, he remains beloved today and is Ireland's patron saint. On March 17, his special day, wear green in his memory!

Tell me a story about Brigid

Brigid of Kildare was full of stories and life and spirit. She loved all that God had created, and she honored the way the Irish celebrated nature. Through their eyes, she came to love the rugged beauty of the Irish sea, the deep black of the night, and the day-to-day rhythm of sunrise to sunset. Legend has it that before Ireland came to know Christ, fires burned in honor of pagan gods. When Brigid started her community at Kildare, she declared that fire was the light of Christ and that it would bring new life to Ireland.

Every day a monk or a nun would ensure that the fire stayed alive: cracking, sizzling, smoking with warmth and heat. When Brigid died in 470, the flames burned, uninterrupted, for over 1,000 years, until monasteries were destroyed during the Reformation. In 1933, the fire was relit by Brigid's Order and continues to burn to this day.

Brigid was known for her great work among Ireland's poor and her labor as an evangelist—one who shares the good news of Jesus. As her community engaged in Bible study and taking care of God's Holy Word, she shared food and milk with lepers and outcasts, cured the sick, and healed the blind. She was said to have an inexhaustible supply of butter that she would give to anyone who asked. Her joy was in seeing those around her well fed and nourished in soul, spirit, and body. Like Patrick, she continues to be honored and loved in Ireland today. It is said that the ashes of Patrick and Brigid are buried together and that they continue to protect the Irish people, whom they loved so dearly.

Let's talk

Patrick and Brigid were teachers who helped other people learn about God. Who are some people that have helped you learn about God? What are some of the things they have taught you?

Patrick and Brigid used everyday things like plants and light to help teach people about God. What are some everyday things that can help you to remember God and God's love?

Patrick and Brigid are very important to the people of Ireland. Do you know where your family is from? Are there certain saints who are important to your heritage?

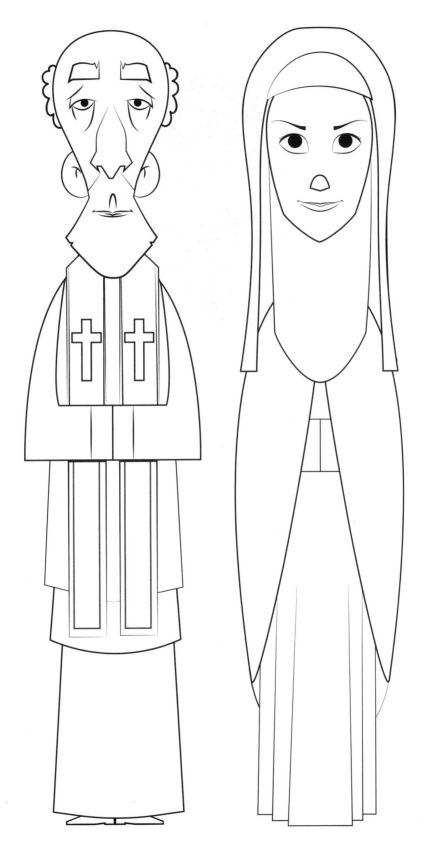

Patrick & Brigid

Augustine of Hippo

Lord God, the light of the minds that know you, the life of the souls that love you, and the strength of the hearts that serve you: Help us, following the example of your servant **Augustine of Hippo**, so to know you that we may truly love you, and so to love you that we may fully serve you, whom to serve is perfect freedom; through Jesus Christ our Lord, who lives and reigns with you and the Holy Spirit, one God, now and for ever. **Amen.** (*Lesser Feasts and Fasts*, p. 361)

Tell me a story

Sometimes our feelings can be like thunderstorms, full of rage and passion, violence and fury. Other times they can be like soft summer winds: peaceful and soothing.

Augustine of Hippo knew both those extremes. As a young man in northern Africa in the third century, he partied loudly, had too many girlfriends, and swore often. His mother, Monnica, was dreadfully worried about him. No matter what she did and how much she prayed, her son seemed terribly out of reach.

Despite his love for parties, Augustine was a top student. He drank up books like they were water, always thirsty for knowledge. Philosophy and law were favorite subjects. He grew up and became a professor, teaching the subject of rhetoric (re-tore-rick), which is the study of how best to use language to influence others.

Yet words, despite their power, can be empty. Augustine's strong mind and nimble soul kept pushing him to ask deep questions. What is God like? Who is this man called Jesus that I've heard so much about? If he loves me and wants the best from me, what does that mean for the way I act? All the while, his mom kept praying that her son would come closer to Jesus.

Finally, in his early thirties, Augustine began the process of study that would lead to his baptism. In those days, most people weren't baptized as babies. Adults were allowed to present themselves for baptism only after long periods of reading the Bible, asking deep questions, and meditating on the nature of God. And Augustine, more than many others, needed that time.

Pacing back and forth in his garden one day, he longed for clarity. Questions about faith and God flooded his brain like spring rains. A brilliant thinker, he would not reduce his faith to simple yes and no answers. And it was in that moment of intense inner dialogue that a child's voice over the garden wall broke through the stillness with four simple words: "Take up and read." Augustine believed that God was speaking to him through that child's voice, and he wanted to obey.

Opening his Bible, he read the first thing he saw: "Let us live honorably as in the day, not in reveling and drunkenness, not in debauchery and licentiousness, not in quarreling and jealously. Instead, put on the Lord Jesus Christ, and make no provision for the flesh, to gratify its desires (Romans 13:13-14).

The words spoke straight to him. Augustine was ready. He asked to be baptized, and his life turned around. With as much passion as he had brought to living wildly, he put aside everything else and became a great church leader, writer, and bishop, one who deeply influenced the Christian church, even unto this very day.

Let's talk

Consider your baptism. Have you been baptized? Do you remember? Who are your godparents? Where were you baptized? In the service of Holy Baptism, we pray that those we are baptizing might have "an inquiring and discerning heart." How is that true of Augustine? What does that mean for you?

Have you ever been told that you ask too many questions? How did it feel to hear that? Why is it important to ask questions about our faith?

God wants to know everything that is on our minds. How do you best share what's on your mind with God?

John of Damascus

Confirm our minds, O Lord, in the mysteries of the true faith, set forth with power by your servant **John of Damascus**; that we, with him, confessing Jesus to be true God and true Man, and singing the praises of the risen Lord, may, by the power of the resurrection, attain to eternal joy; through Jesus Christ our Lord, who lives and reigns with you and the Holy Spirit, one God, now and for ever. **Amen.** (*Lesser Feasts and Fasts*, p. 93)

Tell me a story

Whether we're young or old, most of us don't like fighting. The saints of God faced that same problem. They didn't like fights either, but because they stood up for Jesus, they often landed right in the middle of big conflicts.

John of Damascus was no exception. Born into a prominent Christian family in the Muslim town of Damascus, Syria, John chose to be a monk at about age forty, close to the year 740 CE. Monks live simple but deep lives: they pray, write, grow food, study, and worship God. They promise to live a life of poverty, to stay single, and to do what God and their leader tells them to do. Their first job is prayer, and because they live so deliberately, they are said to live a contemplative lifestyle.

Knowing that prayer takes many different forms, John wrote magnificent poetry, deep theological essays, and beautiful hymns. On Easter Day, two of his hymns, "Come, Ye Faithful, Raise the Strain" and "The Day of Resurrection! Earth Tell It Out Abroad!" are still sung at many churches around the world.

Like John, his fellow monks looked deeply into themselves to find the best way to express God's love. Some meditated for hours. Others copied and illustrated Bible passages. All spent considerable time on their knees in prayer. Monks believe that we can discover God, not only by looking out at the world God made and at Jesus, but also by looking deeply within ourselves as well. That is part of why monks pray so much.

In such times, where God is close and the human spirit is receptive, brilliant art and literary forms often emerge. In John's monastery and others, monks created icons: a special art form where the artist carefully draws and then paints a picture of Jesus, Mary, the disciples, or their followers. If you've looked at a painting in a museum, or spent time creating a painting yourself, you know the energy and thought that goes into such work.

Unfortunately for John and for his fellow monks, the Iconoclastic Controversy (Eye-conno-clastic Con-tro-versie) exploded onto the world stage right at that time. Known as "breakers of images," the Iconoclasts demanded that all such images were to be destroyed. Their reasoning? The second commandment that God gave to Moses said that God's people were not to worship any graven images, just God.

John came to the rescue, with carefully thought-out theological reasons. He said that to draw strength from such images is a way of growing closer to God, not farther away. He knew that objects that bring people closer to God was not the same as worshiping the object itself. And even though he was Christian, he was protected by the Muslim community in his right to practice his religion as he saw fit.

John lived a long and full life and died at the age of seventy-four. Looking back, he must have seen the pieces of his life all fit together: a Christian upbringing, life in Muslim community, the influence of the East, a community in which to grow and to express his thoughts, the love of fellow monks, and the expression of God's love in artistic and intellectual work.

John of Damascus had lived a very good life indeed, and he touches our lives still, every time we sing one of his Easter hymns.

Let's talk

Two of John's famous hymns that we sing in church every Easter season are: "Come, ye faithful, raise the strain," (*The Hymnal 1982*, #199, #200) and "The day of resurrection! Earth tell it out abroad!" (#210). Do you recognize those hymns? Perhaps a musically inclined person could play or sing the hymns for you. Remember that they are about 1,300 years old and written by a person who loved Jesus a great deal.

Consider in your mind a simple picture of your parents or grandparents. You know that the picture is not them, yet it helps you think of them; it helps you see them. How is that like looking at an icon?

Hildegard of Bingen

God of all times and seasons: Give us grace that we, after the example of your servant **Hildegard**, may both know and make known the joy and jubilation of being part of your creation, and show forth your glory not only with our lips but in our lives; through Jesus Christ our Savior, who lives and reigns with you and the Holy Spirit, one God, for ever and ever. **Amen.** (*Lesser Feasts and Fasts*, p. 383)

Tell me a story

Have you ever seen a picture of the ocean? Oceans look beautiful and majestic in pictures or on TV. But have you ever seen the ocean up close...touched it, smelled it, felt its power and its size? An ocean is much different in person. You can walk and play along its edge, or you might fly over it and look at it, but it's so deep in places that no one has ever been to the bottom of it.

Or consider campfires. On TV, they look interesting, no doubt. But when you stand next to them, you will see crackling and hissing and have to jump back if you get too close. They can whip up and burn out of control on a moment's notice—or they can be so tame that you can toast marshmallows over them.

Some people have a tendency to treat God like a tame fire or a placid ocean. But like both, God isn't someone we can box in, or even fully define. We know that God is love, but God's love is bigger and deeper than the universe...and the universe is bigger than we can even imagine.

Hildegard of Bingen, a famous mystic, writer, and healer who was born in 1098 in Germany, understood and expressed the depths of God better than just about anyone. For most of her life, she saw dazzling visions of God and Jesus: brilliant, colorful, musical, life-changing images in three dimensions. But not knowing what people would think, she kept her visions locked tightly inside.

When she was eight years old, her parents sent her to live with a woman named Jetta, an anchorite (ang-KUH-rahyt). Anchorites lived their whole life in a very small room, like a prison cell, where they would pray and chant prayers. Such a commitment was seen as a noble profession...but apparently for her (and thankfully for us), God did not think it the right vocation for Hildegaard.

At age fifteen, Hildegard committed herself to being a Benedictine nun. Like other monastics, she devoted herself in prayer and study to God, committing to a life of poverty, chastity (remaining single), and obedience. When she was thirty-eight years old, she was elected as abbess, or leader, of the women. And then five years later, she experienced a turning point in her life.

Hildegard told of the brilliant vision she had seen, and the words she had heard: "O fragile one, ash of ash and corruption of corruption, say and write what you see." And from that point, that's just what Hildegard did. Over the next ten years, she recorded hundreds of visions—ones that she had seen for years but was scared to share. No longer did she have to keep them bottled up within her. No longer would she stumble under their intensity.

She was a visionary, to be sure. She was also a poet, composer, theologian, playwright, doctor, and twelfth-century pharmacist, developing over 200 herbal remedies. She even wrote about healing people from cancer—a disease that stymies doctors today.

Religious leaders, including the Pope, respected her and sought her opinion. At age sixty-five, she began a four-part preaching tour, which was highly unusual (and wonderful) for a woman to undertake.

Hildegaard knew that God is not always understandable and is much deeper than we can know. And that is like Hildegaard herself, for she developed a coded language of over 900 words, with an alphabet of twenty-three letters. To this day, no one has been able to successfully crack the code.

When Hildegard died, at the age of eighty-one, her sisters reported that a bright light from heaven in the shape of a cross passed over their convent. Was it Hildegard joining her beloved Jesus in heaven? Or was it Jesus coming to hold her in his arms and see her safely home? Like her secret language, no one knows for sure. What we do know is this: the world is a far better place because of artists and creative thinkers like Hildegard of Bingen.

Let's talk

What do you think was the main message of Hildegard's visions?

Sometimes it is hard to see things differently than other people do. What can Hildegard teach us about the value of the arts in our life of faith?

Hildegard used her talents and gifts to tell other people about God. What do you think you're particularly good at? How can you use your skills and gifts to tell people about God and Jesus?

Hildegard of Bingen

Clare of Assisi

O God, whose blessed Son became poor that we through his poverty might be rich: Deliver us from an inordinate love of this world, that we, inspired by the devotion of your servant **Clare**, may serve you with singleness of heart, and attain to the riches of the age to come; through Jesus Christ our Lord, who lives and reigns with you and the Holy Spirit, one God, for ever and ever. **Amen.** (*Lesser Feasts and Fasts*, p. 341)

Tell me a story

The frantic sounds of battle—horses neighing, soldiers shouting, swords being unleashed—awoke Sister Clare, an ill forty-year-old woman. Not that she was sleeping much these days, for the battle outside her walls had been raging for days. But tonight was different. Enemy warriors were on the move, preparing to climb up the walls of her small home. Within a few minutes, they could be smashing windows and doors, drawing knives to the throats of Clare and her sisters.

And these were no normal set of sisters. Clare and her companions lived in community, as if they were sisters, doing all they could to serve the poor in Jesus' name. They went barefoot, slept on the floor, lived only on what others shared with them, and did not marry or have children so that they could stay focused on their work.

In that moment Clare stood tall. She knew what she must do. She would call on God. Praying as she sped down a dark hallway, Clare thought of the night so long ago that had changed everything. Her father had wanted her to marry, yet she had heard another voice calling her: the voice of God. She had run away one night, much like this one, to join the work of Francis, a monk and servant of the poor who was her friend. He had inspired her like no other.

Clare entered a small chapel, where the women gathered up to seven times a day to pray and sing hymns of praise. Quickly she found what she sought: bread and wine blessed by a priest and set aside.

Once back in her room, she marched bravely to the small window that overlooked the little town. And then she did what a priest at an altar does: she held the bread up as a sign of Jesus' presence and protection.

The soldiers fled.

Was it the presence of the Body and Blood of Christ? Was it something else? Clare did not know what the next day would bring, but she knew this much: that she would give it all to God.

She went back to bed and became strong and healthy again, to work for Jesus.

Let's talk

Clare's given name was *Chiara*, the Italian word for bright light. She was indeed a bright light for many. What is the story behind your name? How might you be a bright light for others?

Clare's father had planned a traditional life for her of marriage and children, but God had other things in mind for her, and she listened to God. What might God be calling you to do with your life?

Clare held up the Body of Christ to frighten the enemy, yet it was bread blessed by a priest that she was holding in her hands. Have you seen a priest bless bread and wine on Sunday morning? How is Jesus with us in that moment, and in that bread?

Martin Luther

O God, our refuge and our strength: You raised up your servant **Martin Luther** to reform and renew your Church in the light of your word. Defend and purify the Church in our own day and grant that, through faith, we may boldly proclaim the riches of your grace which you have made known in Jesus Christ our Savior, who with you and the Holy Spirit, lives and reigns, one God, now and for ever. **Amen.** (*Lesser Feasts and Fasts*, p. 173)

Tell me a story

Have you ever been so scared so that you were shaking, almost unable to move? That kind of fear and trembling struck a young man named Martin Luther in Germany some 500 years ago—and it had worldwide ramifications.

Here's what happened: Martin's father had decided that his son should be a lawyer. Lawyers are helpful to have in a family, and they usually earn good money. But a trip home from visiting his family changed his life. Martin climbed aboard his faithful horse and started the trip back to school. Peaceful clouds overhead began acting like angry warriors, thrusting and parrying, using every available tool—thunder, lightening, hail, and hurricane-strength winds—to blast the world apart. Or so it seemed to Martin.

When a fierce lightening bolt seemed to lunge right for him, a prayer burst from his lips: "Help, Saint Anna, I will become a monk!" (Saint Anna is the Blessed Virgin Mary's mother and Jesus' grandmother.) Martin kept his promise, taking standard monastic vows of poverty, chastity, and obedience—and leaving his father outraged.

But God must have known that Martin's voice was desperately needed to set things right. As sometimes happens with institutions, the Roman Catholic Church had fallen on hard times, and clergy were doing terrible things. Some priests were accepting money to supposedly offer forgiveness to people who had already died, even if the people had committed terrible sins when they were alive.

The fact that clergy were accepting this kind of payout enraged Martin Luther, who knew that the Church's main mission was to help the common man and woman and to take care of those whom Jesus would serve first: the poor and the outcast. And Martin knew something else as well: we can't earn our way to heaven based on our behavior. We are granted eternal life through our faith, our trust in God's love for us. No amount of good deeds by themselves can do the trick.

In a surge of anger toward the Church's poor leadership, Martin nailed 95 points of belief—known as "theses"—to the heavy wooden doors at the castle church in Wittenburg. It was like broadcasting his thoughts on the Internet, as a challenge. "Here I stand," he said, according to those who knew and loved him. "Here I stand, for I can do no other."

His brave words encouraged other scholars to step forth and help the Church change its ways. Like breaking waves on a beach, what was positive about the Church stayed, and what was negative washed away, all across Europe and England. Because of the Protestant Reformation and the invention of the printing press, people were finally able to read the Bible for themselves, approach God directly, and recover the joy of faith.

So the next time you feel yourself scared, and want to change course on something you are doing, listen carefully, as did Martin. It just may be the voice of the Holy Spirit talking—and the Spirit may have important work for you to do too.

Let's talk

Martin Luther dedicated much of his life to making sure that ordinary people could read the Bible. Do you read the Bible? When and how? What is your favorite Bible story? Why do you like it?

Martin Luther thought it was important to use both our hearts and our minds to help us know the right thing to do. How can you listen to your heart when making tough decisions? How can you use your mind?

Have you ever been as scared as Martin was? Did any good come out of it? If so, what?

Thomas Cranmer

Keep us, O Lord, constant in faith and zealous in witness, that, like your servants Hugh Latimer, Nicholas Ridley, and **Thomas Cranmer**, we may live in your fear, die in your favor, and rest in your peace; for the sake of Jesus Christ your Son our Lord, who lives and reigns with you and the Holy Spirit, one God, now and for ever. **Amen.** (*Lesser Feasts and Fasts*, p. 421)

Tell me a story

Picture a very dark night. Perhaps you've been camping and know how dark it is outside in the woods at night. Or think of your room when all the lights are off—it's hard to see anything! Now visualize a candle in that space—instantly things are different. You can see; you know where you are, all is clear.

Saints are like that: lights in a dark world. They fight evil powers because they follow the brightest light of all: Jesus. Their faith burns brightest especially when all seems lost, and they light the way for us, even centuries later.

Thomas Cranmer of England was one of those great light-bearing saints, although it came at great expense to him. He spoke English—albeit an old-fashioned English, full of words like "thee" and "thou" and "mayest" and "holpen." And he lived in a dangerous time we call the Protestant Reformation.

When we go to church on Sunday, much of what we actually say is because of Thomas. That's because he was what we call the "architect" of our *Book of Common Prayer*. Architects take ideas and raw materials and put them together to make buildings. Thomas built the first *Book of Common Prayer* in 1549 by masterfully weaving together ancient prayers and hymns, Bible readings, and his own, beautifully written, new prayers.

It was as if he and the other Protestant reformers, Martin Luther from Germany and John Calvin from Switzerland, were building a beautiful new garden for the Church: a garden where Christians could stroll with Jesus and sit down and talk to him, one-on-one. Before then, church services had been in Latin, not the language of the people. Some top church leaders were corrupt, promising things they could not give. Thomas and the others worked to pull the bad weeds so that all would be clean and new.

Yet evil lurked right outside the walls of that garden. Thomas had served as Archbishop of Canterbury and advised King Henry VIII, who desperately wanted a son to survive him on the throne. King Henry is known in history for marrying eight different women in search of that healthy son. Thomas struggled to help him but was tossed like a ship at sea during political and religious chaos in England.

When King Henry died, Thomas was at his bedside, ever the loyal companion. England's next successor to the throne was a woman that neither Henry nor Thomas wanted: Henry's daughter, Mary. Within a few short months, Thomas was a marked man. Queen Mary, known as Bloody Mary, had Thomas imprisoned, and eventually burned at the stake in Oxford.

Despite the flames, and perhaps because of them, Thomas stood up even more strongly for his beliefs and for the Lord Jesus Christ. Quoting Saint Stephen, a young man who had been killed for his faith shortly after the death of Jesus, Thomas called out: "Lord Jesus, receive my spirit...I see heavens opened and Jesus standing at the right hand of God."

Thomas' great gift to the church was in crafting beautiful prayers for all to say together. It is said that because of his work, angels and archangels in heaven sing more clearly, and more in unison, than ever before.

Let's talk

What stands out for you about Thomas Cranmer? What questions might you have about him? Or, if you were talking with him, what would you ask him?

Why is it important for people to pray in the language they know best? What languages do people in your family speak? Are they different or the same as the ones you and your friends use?

Do you have a favorite prayer from *The Book of Common Prayer*? What is it and why do you love it?

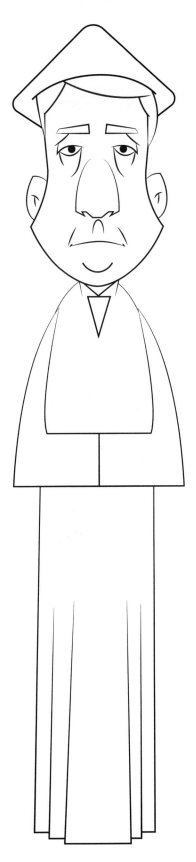

Thomas Cranmer

George Herbert

Our God and King, you called your servant **George Herbert** from the pursuit of worldly honors to be a pastor of souls, a poet, and a priest in your temple: Give us grace, we pray, joyfully to perform the tasks you give us to do, knowing that nothing is menial or common that is done for your sake; through Jesus Christ our Lord, who lives and reigns with you and the Holy Spirit, one God, for ever and ever. **Amen.** (*Lesser Feasts and Fasts*, p. 179)

Tell me a story

As night settled in on the small village of Bemerton, England, George Herbert—pastor, poet, and priest—could have done what most townspeople did: sit before his warm hearth and turn into bed early. But George was a writer, and he did what writers must do: he put pen to paper and wrote.

Listen to the poetry that flowed from his soul:

King of glory, King of peace, I will love thee
and that love may never cease, I will move thee.
Thou hast granted my request, thou has heard me
and those didst note my working breast, thou has spared me.

Seven whole days, not one in seven, I will praise thee;
in my heart, though not in heaven, I will raise thee.
Small it is in this poor sort to enroll thee,
e'en eternity's too short to extol thee.
(The Hymnal 1982, #382)

By day, George did what clergy do: he visited the sick and prayed with them, baptized babies, buried the dead, preached, and led worship on both weekdays and on Sunday. And by all accounts, this work gave him great joy and helped him enter more deeply into his writing. He wasn't just writing into empty space. He was writing about how God's love transformed his life and the lives of those he served.

Ordained to the priesthood at the relatively late age of thirty-six, he could have been a professor at Trinity College in Cambridge, where he had been a brilliant student and orator, speaking for the community on public occasions. Or he could have been a lifetime member of Parliament, where he had served for two years.

Yet something was pulling at his heart. And that something was the life of writing. God was calling him into a life of reflection as both priest and writer. Answering that call in a small parish, among country people, George composed hundreds of written pieces, including a number of poems and hymns that are popular today.

George died at the age of thirty-nine from tuberculosis. Fortunately, just before his death, he turned his masterpiece, *The Temple*, over to his good friend Nicholas Ferrar.

"If you think these poems might help any poor dejected soul, see if you can get them published." George said. "And if not, burn them!"

Thankfully Nicholas Ferrar realized the value of his friend's poems and published them as soon as he could.

Close your eyes now and listen to the words of George Herbert, a priest, pastor, and poet. And if you have an organist or musician among you, play the music as you sing, for we find this hymn in our hymnal as well.

Come, my Way, my Truth, my Life:
such a way as gives us breath;
such a truth as ends all strife;
such a life as killeth death.

Come, my Light, my Feast, my Strength:
such a light as shows a feast;
such a feast as mends in length;
such a strength as makes his guest.

Come, my Joy, my Love, my Heart:
such a joy as none can move; such a love as none can part;
such a heart as joys in love.
(The Hymnal 1982, #487)

Let's talk

Do you like to write? Or paint? Or draw? Or play music? How can those gifts be a sign of God working in you?

Is there a hymn, song, or poem that makes you feel close to God (it doesn't have to be "religious")? What is it and how does it draw you near to God?

There were a lot of different things that George Herbert could have done, but he felt God "tugging at his heart" and that guided his path. Have you ever felt God tugging at your heart? What was that like?

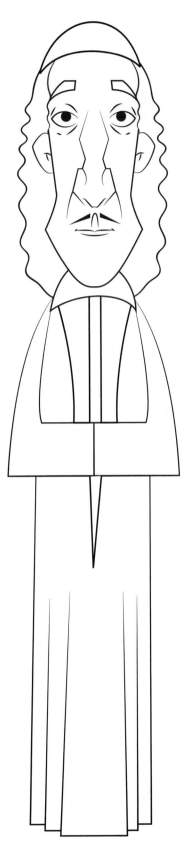

George Herbert

Johann Sebastian Bach

Almighty God, beautiful in majesty and majestic in holiness, who teaches us in Holy Scripture to sing your praises and who gave your musicians **Johann Sebastian Bach**, George Frederick Handel and Henry Purcell grace to show forth your glory in their music: Be with all those who write or make music for your people, that we on earth may glimpse your beauty and know the inexhaustible riches of your new creation in Jesus Christ our Savior; who lives and reigns with you and the Holy Spirit, one God, for ever and ever. **Amen.** (*Holy Women, Holy Men*, p. 491)

Tell me a story

Pretend that you are in a beautiful old Lutheran church in the small town of Leipzig, Germany, in the eighteenth century. Stretching across the red brick floor are beautiful color panels, thrown down by the early morning sun pouring through stained glass windows. Roosters crow outside. Church bells toll. And then, as a blast of organ music seems to shake the building, you realize you are not alone.

Looking up toward the organ loft, you see a white-haired man. Now he is playing soft and melodic sounds, now wild and discordant notes. He stops. He scribbles. He talks to himself. He hums. And then he is at it again: a cadence of music, writing, singing, sighing, and more music.

A piece of paper flutters down from the loft, full of handwritten musical notes, signed with the initials: "S.D.G." You wonder: What's the man's name? Who could S.D.G. be?

And then the door to the sacristy opens. In walks a priest, to whom you hand the paper.

"Do you know who's up there?" he asks. You shake your head.

"That's our church musician, Johann Sebastian Bach," the priest says. "But he signs 'S.D.G' on most of his church music. In Latin it means, *Soli Deo Gloria*...Glory to God alone."

"Good morning, Mr. Bach," the priest waves up. "Just some simple church music tomorrow? You know, just regular Sunday church music."

The eighth child in a musical family, Johann soaked up music like a young oak tree. He grew to be one of the most famous composers in the history of the world. Nearly all of his music was written for use in churches.

Brilliant artists are not always appreciated in their own time, and Bach was no exception. His creative music did not always fit what people were expecting on a Sunday morning. But when it was all done, Bach followed the voice within him, and this voice has lasted. Most importantly, Johann Sebastian Bach understood what and who he was creating for: *Soli Deo Gloria*. Glory to God alone.

Let's talk

When you engage in your favorite activity, how do you ask God to be a part of it? How might you dedicate your activities to God, like J.S. Bach did?

Bach wrote his music "S.D.G.", for God's glory alone. How might we offer the music we sing or play in church only to God's glory?

Twenty hymns in The Episcopal Church hymnal were composed by Johann Sebastian Bach. One of the most famous is "A Mighty Fortress is our God" (Hymns 687, 888). The words were written by Martin Luther, the Lutheran theologian that was Bach's greatest influence. Grab a hymnal and read along. Or sing along, if possible. What do you think is the most important theme? How do the words complement the music?

Charles Wesley

Lord God, you inspired your servants John and **Charles Wesley** with burning zeal for the sanctification of souls, and endowed them with eloquence in speech and song: Kindle in your Church, we entreat you, such fervor, that those whose faith has cooled may be warmed, and those who have not known Christ may turn to him and be saved; who lives and reigns with you and the Holy Spirit, one God, now and for ever. **Amen.** (*Lesser Feasts and Fasts*, p. 187)

Tell me a story

Have you learned to ride a bike? Have you planted a garden? Have you studied really hard for a particular test at school? Have you cared for a dog or a cat or a fish?

If so, you would probably agree that success does not happen within a few minutes. You need to feed dogs and train them over time. Riding a bike takes practice. Gathering—and eating—vegetables from a garden takes planting, watering, weeding, and harvesting. And being good at school means doing the hard work, day after day, and year after year.

And sometimes, as hard as you work at something, it may not go the way you want. Sometimes animals die, despite our love and care for them. Sometimes we fall off our bikes. Sometimes gardens wither away or weeds overtake them. And even if you've studied hard at school, you may not be good at a particular subject.

It was like that for Charles Wesley back in eighteenth-century England. Born into a family of nineteen children (he was the eighteenth child), he and his brother John were faithful and dedicated members of Christ Church, Oxford. Gathering regularly with his friends for Holy Communion, Bible study, and prayer, Charles and his friends were teased by other students—snidely called "Methodists"— because they were so methodical in prayer.

Yet because they loved God, they persevered, using an early edition of the very *Book of Common Prayer* that we use in The Episcopal Church today. Following in the footsteps of their father, Charles and John were ordained as priests in the Church of England and then set out for the United States as missionaries.

Their high hopes, however, were soon dashed. Their message was not heard in America, and they returned to England within a few years. Yet their faith in Jesus continued to burn strong within them.

On Pentecost Sunday—May 21 in 1738—Charles felt what he described as "heart palpitations." John felt the same sensation within several days. Their faith told them that it was God speaking within them, turning their already-warm hearts for God into burning hearts. Enlivened by a new wave of energy, Charles and John preached across England, especially to those on the margins of society: the working poor, the homeless, and those in poverty. They still believed in deep practices of prayer and study, known as The Method, but at the heart of their faith was a personal relationship with Jesus and his ability to change every human heart.

Preaching their faith in every field and factory possible, Charles and John Wesley led a massive revival in England. And Charles did more than preach. One of the greatest hymn composers of all time, he wrote over 6,000 hymns, many of which are sung in churches today, including The Episcopal Church. Charles knew that hymns brought people closer to God by speaking to our hearts through music and poetry combined.

Though Charles remained a faithful member of the Church of England until the day he died, his vision and energy also gave birth to the Methodist Church, which now, in various forms, numbers more than 100 million members around the world.

Charles Wesley's faith was not born on that fateful day when he felt his heart race. He had prepared the way for Jesus through years of prayer, Bible study, and reflection with other Christians. He had experienced years of difficult times in his ministry and taunting from fellow students.

Yet he kept the flames of faith tended in his heart—and from them, God was able to bring forth a blazing fire, one that would inspire millions of people around the world to know and love God. As Charles said so well in one of his hymns: "Faith, mighty faith, the promise sees; and looks to God alone; Laughs at impossibilities, and cries it shall be done."

Let's talk

What is one of your favorite hymns that we sing in church? What do you like about it?

Charles Wesley kept working at his faith until it blossomed for him. What is something you've worked hard at, and perhaps had a setback or two, before it came alive for you?

Charles Wesley's brother John was an important partner for him in his life of faith. Who are some friends or family members that are important partners in your life of faith? What do they do to support you?

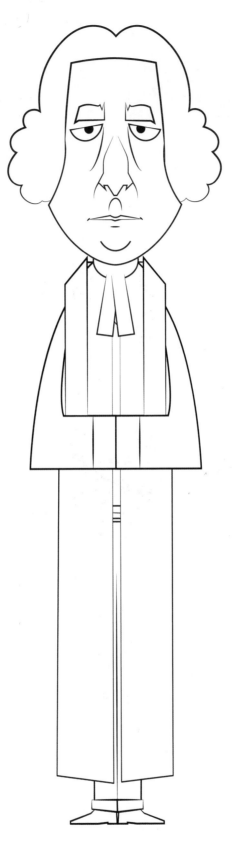

Charles Wesley

Samuel Seabury

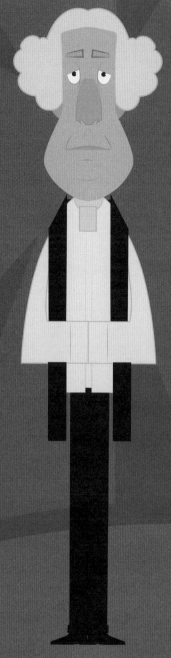

We give you thanks, O Lord our God, for your goodness in bestowing upon this Church the gift of the episcopate, which we celebrate in this remembrance of the consecration of **Samuel Seabury**; and we pray that, joined together in unity with our bishops, and nourished by your holy Sacraments, we may proclaim the Gospel of redemption with apostolic zeal; through Jesus Christ our Lord, who lives and reigns with you and the Holy Spirit, one God, now and for ever. **Amen.** (*Lesser Feasts and Fasts,* p. 453)

Tell me a story

Have you ever seen a bishop? Bishops are an important part of The Episcopal Church. And for that matter, so are you.

Our church family works a bit like your own extended family. You might have cousins, or brothers, or sisters. You were born to parents. And somewhere back there, whether you have known them or not, are your grandparents and great-grandparents. Everyone has a part to play, and everyone is equally valuable in God's eyes.

In our Episcopal Church family, we have what we call three orders of ordained ministers: bishops, priests, and deacons. Priests bless the bread and wine at the altar and help us remember that Jesus died for us. Deacons remind us to go out into the world and serve others and bring the concerns of the world back to the altar. Bishops ordain people to be priests and deacons, confirm others to be God's everyday agents in the world, and lead dioceses—or groups of churches—so we can all stick together.

The largest group of ministers in the Church, however, is known as the laity. That is about 99 percent of all the members of the Church, which includes YOU! The laity's main job is to make Jesus known in the world: in the workplace, in schools, in hospitals, and at home.

Knowing what you now know, think about when this country was just becoming the United States of America. Like families do sometimes, the country was going through a complicated time.

There were no bishops, and even priests and deacons had to go to England to be ordained. Yet at that time, England and America were fighting with each other. Clergy had to swear allegiance to King George of England, and they were often mistrusted and beaten for their allegiance to England.

For a while, churches just locked their doors, hoping the problem would solve itself. But problems rarely do. As our country grew stronger and more independent, clergy in Connecticut decided that the Church here in America really did need its own bishop. It is good when families can be strong, and they wanted our church family to be strong.

They elected a priest from Connecticut, Samuel Seabury, to go to England and seek ordination. Samuel agreed and sailed off across the rough Atlantic Ocean, putting his future in God's hands. Once in England, however, Samuel was turned down by English bishops because he would not swear allegiance to King George.

Samuel, however, would not be put off. He believed that God had called him to make the new church strong in America. Eventually he found his way to Scotland, and because Scotland was not happy with Britain at the time either, several bishops there were pleased to ordain Samuel Seabury as America's first bishop.

Tensions were still strong when Samuel arrived home—but The Episcopal Church in America was standing now on its own two feet, much like the new young United States of America. Over the years, England and the United States grew to be close friends, or allies, and The Episcopal Church in America grew stronger as well. Today there are over 300 active bishops in the Church doing the job they are called to do: ordaining, confirming, and leading.

Let's talk

Have you ever seen the bishop at your church? What do you remember about the bishop's visit?

The mitre is one of the symbols of the bishop; another symbol is the crozier, or bishop's staff. A bishop's staff is shaped like a shepherd's crook. That's because bishops are like shepherds, who lead their flocks on behalf of Jesus, the Great Shepherd. Have you ever seen a shepherd with a sheep? Why are Christians compared to sheep in God's eyes?

We heard in Samuel Seabury's story that everyone has a part to play in the church family. What do you think is your part to play in our church family?

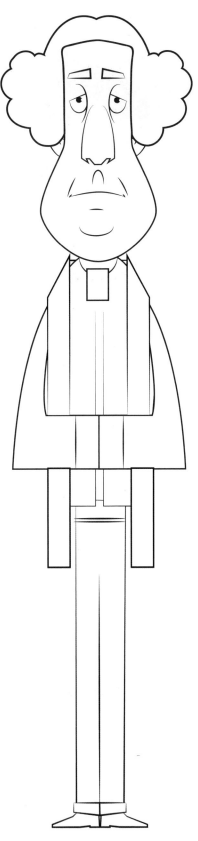

Samuel Seabury

Enmegahbowh

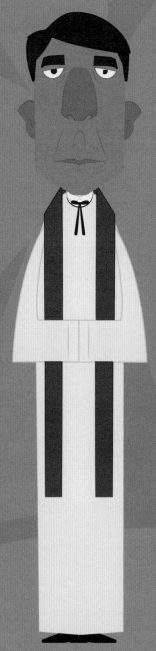

Almighty God, you led your pilgrim people of old with fire and cloud: Grant that the ministers of your Church, following the example of blessed **Enmegahbowh**, may stand before your holy people, leading them with fiery zeal and gentle humility. This we ask through Jesus, the Christ, who lives and reigns with you in the unity of the Holy Spirit, one God now and for ever. **Amen.** (*Lesser Feasts and Fasts*, p. 285)

Tell me a story

What should have been a pleasant sail that day on Lake Superior for Enmegahbowh (N-muh-gab-bwah), and his wife, Iron Sky Woman, was anything but calm. Each wave seemed to scream its own warning. Risk! Peril! Chaos!

Despite the danger, however, Enmegahbowh knew he had made the right decision. Trained as a medicine man for his Ottawa tribe in Canada and brought up as a Christian with Methodist roots, he worked as a missionary in the upper Midwest. Most recently, he had operated a small mission school for Native children in northern Minnesota—but then discovered the Methodists planned to abandon their mission work.

Discouraged, he decided to return home. Surely God could use him there. With each minute the waves grew bigger and more menacing. Flinging the boat around like barn cats do with mice, the waves seemed intent on crashing the vessel—and casting its trembling passengers into the frigid waters.

In that moment, looking into the jaws of death, Enmegahbowh heard a voice. "Ah, my friend Enmegahbowh, I know you," it said. "You are a fugitive. You have sinned and disobeyed God. Instead of going to the city of Nineveh, where God sent you to spread his word to the people, you started to go, and then turned aside. You are now on your way to the city of Tarshish….'"

Enmegahbowh knew at once to whom the voice belonged: the Old Testament prophet Jonah, swallowed by a whale himself while running away from work God had called him to do—preach the word of God in the far-away city of Tarshish. But Jonah didn't want to go to there, for the people had been known to be evil and murderous. After three days, God caused the whale to spit out Jonah onto a beach. Straightaway, the prophet went to Tarshish—and his words were well received.

I hear you, God, thought Enmegahbowh. I hear you. Like Jonah, Enmegahbowh listened—and reversed his course. Upon embarking, he met the Rev. Josiah Gear, who welcomed him into The Episcopal Church, giving him *The Book of Common Prayer*. Josiah also introduced him to Bishop James Lloyd Breck, who was planting churches throughout the West.

Enmegahbowh was soon ordained to the priesthood, the first recognized Native American priest in the United States. Committed to the cause of nonviolence, Enmegahbowh worked as a bridge between the Native American community and those who were new to this country. Brave and stalwart, he saved the lives of those in both communities—and suffered for this as well, for it is hard being a peace worker.

Enmegahbowh's work among the Native Americans was legendary. He oversaw the development of biblical and worship material in Ojibway, and he helped build strong communities of faith throughout northern Minnesota and adjacent states. After fifty-four years of working among his people, Enmegahbowh died at the age of ninety-five, full of years, and a faithful minister of Jesus Christ. Like the prophet Jonah, Enmegahbowh did what God wanted him to do...and the world was a better place for it.

Let's talk

The story of Jonah was very important to Enmegahbowh. What is your favorite Bible story? What character in the Bible do you feel connected to and why?

Enmegahbowh most often referred to God as "the Great Spirit." How might this name help us understand God better?

Enmegahbowh was the first Native American priest in the United States. Have you had the experience of being first at something? What was that like?

C.S. Lewis

O God of searing truth and surpassing beauty, we give you thanks for **Clive Staples Lewis**, whose sanctified imagination lights fires of faith in young and old alike. Surprise us also with your joy and draw us into that new and abundant life which is ours in Christ Jesus, who lives and reigns with you and the Holy Spirit, one God, now and for ever. **Amen.**
(*Lesser Feasts and Fasts*, p. 465)

Tell me a story

Imagine what you would see if you could walk around in the head of C.S. Lewis—one of the greatest writers of the twentieth century. You might see a giant lion named Aslan. You might see a lamppost in the woods, drawing you into one of the greatest book series of all times, *The Chronicles of Narnia*. You might see children named Peter and Lucy and Edward and Susan, fighting a shape-changing white witch.

On the other hand, given C.S. Lewis' day job as an English professor at Oxford and Cambridge, you might hear reflections on playwrights such as Shakespeare and Marlowe and poets like Spenser and Keats. You might hear his thoughts as he meets weekly in an Oxford pub called The Bird and Baby for lunch on Tuesdays with friends, to discuss weighty subjects like trolls, hobbits, theology, imagination, and God.

Ah, God!

Despite being one of the world's most beloved Christian writers, C.S. Lewis declared he was an atheist when he was fifteen years old. An atheist is someone who does not believe in God. Many of us are baptized and sometimes take God for granted. But not C.S.—or Jack, as his friends called him. (C.S. stood for "Clive Staples," which seemed a bit formal for his friends.)

It was all or nothing for him, which is why, when he found his faith fifteen years later, he became one of the most articulate spokesmen for Christianity of the twentieth century: writing books, delivering radio talks, attending church, speaking on moral values based on God's love, and gathering with friends. He describes the night he finally and fully believed, at Magdalen College, part of Oxford University:

"You must picture me alone in that room at Magdalen, night after night, feeling, whenever my mind lifted even for a second from my work, the steady, unrelenting approach of him whom I so earnestly desired not to meet. That which I greatly feared had at last come upon me in the Trinity Term of 1929 I gave in, and admitted that God was God, and knelt and prayed: perhaps, that night, the most dejected and reluctant convert in all England." *(Surprised by Joy)*

A deeply honest writer, C.S. Lewis was not afraid to plunge into the depths of his imagination—and God's very being. He was a writer who was not afraid to ask the hardest questions of God and to turn his heart inside out with searching. C.S. Lewis' words have enlivened the faith and hearts of millions of believers—because he trusted in God's gift to him and to us—that of imagination.

Listen to him describe the subject of faith using—what else?—his imagination:

"Imagine yourself as a living house. God comes in to rebuild that house. At first, perhaps, you can understand what He is doing. He is getting the drains right and stopping the leaks in the roof and so on; you knew that those jobs needed doing and so you are not surprised. But presently He starts knocking the house about in a way that hurts abominably and does not seem to make any sense. What on earth is He up to? The explanation is that He is building quite a different house from the one you thought of - throwing out a new wing here, putting on an extra floor there, running up towers, making courtyards. You thought you were being made into a decent little cottage: but He is building a palace. He intends to come and live in it Himself." *(Mere Christianity)*

let's talk

C.S. Lewis and his friends believed that the stories we read when we are young help shape us, even when we become grown-ups. What are some of your favorite stories? What do they teach you about God—and about yourself?

C.S. Lewis believed that imagination was a gift from God. How do poets and musicians and writers and artists use their imagination to make the world a better place? How do you use yours?

C.S. Lewis changed his mind about God; at first he didn't believe in God, but soon he came to know and love God very, very much. Have you ever changed your mind about something? What was that like?

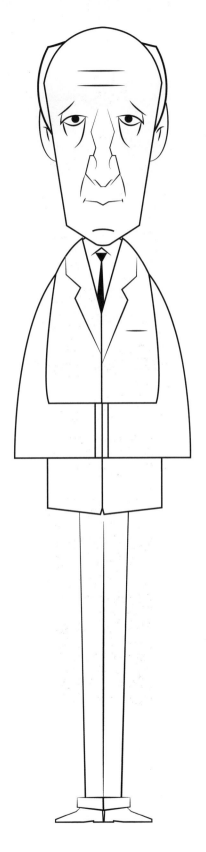

C.S. Lewis

Frances Perkins

Loving God, we bless your Name for **Frances Perkins**, who lived out her belief that the special vocation of the laity is to conduct the secular affairs of society that all may be maintained in health and decency. Help us, following her example, to contend tirelessly for justice and for the protection of all in need, that we may be faithful followers of Jesus Christ; who with you and the Holy Spirit lives and reigns, one God, for ever and ever. **Amen.** (*Holy Women, Holy Men*, p. 243)

Tell me a story

From the time she was a young girl, Frances Perkins noticed things. Born in 1850 into a family in Boston, people told Frances that poor people were responsible for their own poverty. But she watched and noticed that many poor people worked very hard, just as hard as rich people, yet they remained poor. Frances noticed this, and she wondered.

Frances attended Mount Holyoke College in western Massachusetts, graduating with a degree in chemistry and physics. One day in college, Frances visited the textile mills along the Merrimack River north of Boston. In the mill, Frances noticed that the workers were young women her age—yet they didn't get to go to college like she did. As she looked around, Frances noticed that the factory was dangerous and cramped, with too many people working in a small space. Most of the people in this mill worked six or seven days a week, breathing air filled with toxins that made them sick. Frances noticed this, and she wondered.

While getting her master's degree at Columbia University, she joined The Episcopal Church and was confirmed. Then, in New York in 1911, she witnessed a horrific event: the Triangle Shirtwaist Factory Fire, in which almost 150 young women and men died because they were trapped in a burning building and couldn't escape.

For others, it was simply another tragic fire. But as Frances watched, she noticed things. Frances noticed that the doors to the factory were locked, so that the workers couldn't get out when the fire started. Frances noticed that there were no exits or escape routes to keep people safe. Frances noticed that because the workers in the factory were poor, people seemed to think they mattered less. Frances noticed that the poor factory workers had no one to stand up for them.

Frances noticed and wondered. As she noticed, questions gnawed away at her heart. As she wondered, God's Holy Spirit stirred inside her. Frances realized that noticing and wondering was not enough. Frances decided to use her gift for noticing and wondering to do something: she would strive to protect workers from those who would abuse them, she would work to make the lives of the poor better, she would push for the rights of all people. In 1929, Frances Perkins became New York's Commissioner of Labor—the same year as the Great Depression began, a time in which many people went hungry due to lack of jobs.

Frances didn't let tough times stop her. Frances noticed that many people worked hard, but their jobs were dangerous, so she urged workers to gather into unions, and she helped write new safety policies. Frances noticed that sometimes even when people worked hard, they weren't always paid fairly, so Frances helped institute a minimum wage and limit the number of hours in the work week. Frances noticed that children were being forced to work in factories instead of being allowed to go to school and learn, so she helped write laws to end child labor.

Frances Perkins was so good at noticing and wondering and working in New York that in 1933, President Franklin Roosevelt appointed her to be the Secretary of Labor—the first time a woman was appointed to the president's cabinet. Serving for twelve years, she was the main force behind many of the laws that help protect people all over our country today: Social Security; the forty-hour work week, minimum wage, and the law that says if hourly wage earners work more than forty hours, they must be paid extra money.

A woman of prayer and deep faith, Frances spent many weekends on her knees, praying, at a Maryland convent. When Frances noticed something, she prayed to God about it. When Frances wondered about something, she asked Jesus to help her. When Frances began working to change the world, she trusted that it was God's Holy Spirit working in her and through her.

The next time you have a fire drill at school, or hear about your parents paying Social Security taxes, or your grandparents and others receiving Social Security benefits, think of Frances Perkins, and give thanks for her gifts of noticing, and wondering, and working to change the world.

Let's talk

Prayer was very important to Frances Perkins. When do you pray? Does your family have special prayers? What are they?

Frances Perkins believed that even one person could make a difference. What are some things that you can do to help other people at your school? In your neighborhood? At church?

Frances Perkins stood up for other people when no one else was standing up for them. Have you ever seen someone bullied? How did you (or how could you) respond?

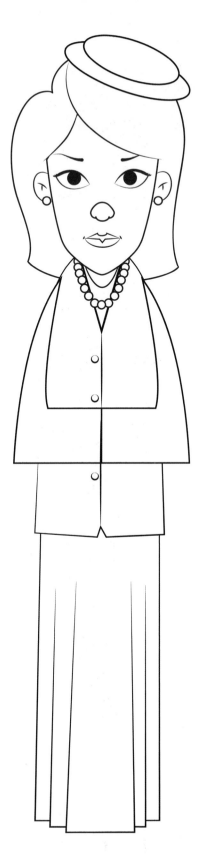

Frances Perkins

Martin Luther King Jr.

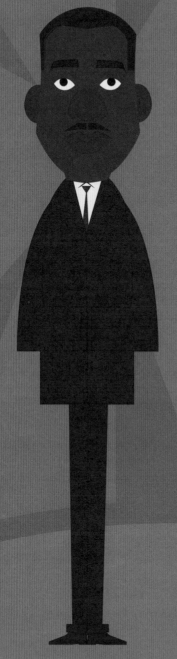

Almighty God, by the hand of Moses your servant you led your people out of slavery, and made them free at last: Grant that your Church, following the example of your prophet **Martin Luther King**, may resist oppression in the name of your love, and may secure for all your children the blessed liberty of the Gospel of Jesus Christ; who lives and reigns with you and the Holy Spirit, one God, now and for ever. **Amen.** (*Lesser Feasts and Fasts*, p. 227)

Tell me a story

Hatred and violence are hard things to understand, especially when God wants us to love each other and strive for peace.

Martin Luther King Jr. was a man who gave his life for peace, even though he knew what it was like to be hated. An African-American, Baptist preacher, and holder of a doctorate degree from Boston University, Martin stood up for others because he knew how wrong it was to be judged on the color of one's skin. Martin grew up in a time when segregation—which means separating people based on their skin color—was practiced routinely. Schools for whites and blacks were separate. Some restaurants refused to serve blacks. People even used different drinking fountains. Housing for many black Americans was substandard, as was education and health care.

Knowing that segregation was wrong, he was determined to change the structures that kept punishing people for their skin color. His work first took him to Montgomery, Alabama, where he served as pastor of Dexter Avenue Baptist Church. At that time, a young woman named Rosa Parks refused to give up her seat on the bus to a white man. In those days, black people had to stand in buses and other public transportation while white people sat down.

Martin knew that wasn't fair, so he and others organized marches and protests to draw attention to the problem of segregation so that people would stop judging others on their skin color. Sometimes the marches became violent, with many black Americans, and some white Americans, getting hurt and killed, but Martin stayed committed to the ways of non-violence and peace. He told people about Jesus, and how Jesus wanted everyone to be treated fairly and equally. And he preached to his followers that dignity and nonviolence was the way forward.

Between 1957 and 1968, Martin Luther King Jr. traveled over six million miles and spoke over 2,500 times. On August 28, 1963, Martin gave a speech to almost a quarter of a million people from the steps of the Lincoln Memorial. He was a leader for what is known as the March on Washington for Jobs and Freedom. And this is what he said:

> I say to you today, my friends, so even though we face the difficulties of today and tomorrow,
> I still have a dream. It is a dream deeply rooted in the American dream.
> I have a dream that one day this nation will rise up and live out the true meaning of its creed:
> "We hold these truths to be self-evident: that all men are created equal."
> I have a dream that one day on the red hills of Georgia the sons of former slaves
> and the sons of former slave owners will be able to sit down together at the table of brotherhood...
> I have a dream that my four little children will one day live in a nation where they
> will not be judged by the color of their skin but by the content of their character.

Sadly, five years later, after many more speeches and marches and sermons, Martin Luther King Jr. was killed by an assassin. Like other saints, however, we know that his brave work and spirit live on, making a difference to this very day—and we trust, through eternity.

Let's talk

Have you ever had an experience where you have been judged by the color of your skin? If so, what was that like?

Do you have any friends with a different skin color than you? Have you ever talked about it? Does it make a difference?

Why is it good to get to know people from different backgrounds? Where is a good place to do that?

Harriet Bedell

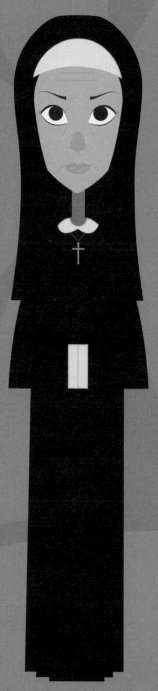

Holy God, you chose your faithful servant **Harriet Bedell** to exercise the ministry of deaconess and to be a missionary among indigenous peoples: Fill us with compassion and respect for all people, and empower us for the work of ministry throughout the world; through Jesus Christ our Lord, who lives and reigns with you and the Holy Spirit, one God, for ever and ever. **Amen.** (*Lesser Feasts and Fasts*, p. 121)

Tell me a story

Some people think that sixty-eight might be considered old. When Harriet Bedell turned sixty-eight, she was told by her bishop that she had to retire. What the bishop didn't know was this: Harriet, one of the toughest people around—and a missionary deacon—had no intention of retiring.

She negotiated with the bishop for her to receive fifty dollars a month in pension payments (almost as much as her monthly salary) and the right to work as long as her health held out. Serving for another seventeen years, she was often heard to say, "There is no retirement in the service of the Master."

Serving the Master, as Harriet so fondly called Jesus, was indeed her passion. She had trained to become a schoolteacher. Until the second half of the twentieth century, teaching was one of the few professions open to women. Yet Harriet's heart burned with a different kind of flame: missionary work among the poor.

Because she was a Christian, she believed that Jesus wanted her to feed the hungry, clothe the naked, visit those in prison, and share the good news about God. Men did those kinds of things routinely, so why not her?

In the past, prophets had worn mantles, or cloaks, that identified them as people who proclaimed God's word. Harriet needed training to put on the full mantle of mission. She began her studies at the New York Training School for Deaconesses, where she could explore theology and the Bible and learn about mission. Women were not allowed to become priests then, nor could they attend seminary. So Harriet took charge, gently forcing open doors that had, until that point, remained closed.

After a yearlong course, she graduated and was sent to the Whirlwind Mission in Oklahoma to serve among the poor. There, she did all she could to care for the sick, educate women and children, and build organizations so people could free themselves from poverty.

Nine years later, the mission closed. Because of her missionary and teaching experience, Harriet was next called to Alaska to serve among the Native population in the tiny and isolated town of Stevens Village. There, Harriet was finally ordained as a deaconess. Today we use the word "deacon" instead. But in 1922, women ordained to that ministry were called deaconesses—and Harriet herself would insist we get her title right. Deaconesses served the poorest of the poor, and were often, like Harriet, very poor themselves.

One more major move for Harriet lay ahead when funds for the Alaska mission also ran short. While on a speaking tour, she visited the Seminole Indian Reservation in southern Florida and knew that was where God desired her to serve. She wasted no time in moving to the Blade Cross Indian Reservation, where she worked for the next thirty years.

Missionaries like Harriet are the best of the best. They don't live in fancy houses while those they serve can barely eat. They don't have three-course meals when simple soup suffices. Harriet lived and worked among the poor, not only helping them to rise above poverty but also working to change systems that kept poverty over their heads like never-ending storm clouds.

Bedell rode her beliefs like a wild stallion—persistently and often into the wind. George Huntoon, an executive with whom she worked, once said, "When the Deaconess got after you for something, I found it was best to acquiesce and comply with her request because she would keep after you until you got it done for her." When Huntoon tried to avoid one of Bedell's requests by creeping down the fire escape, she figured out the deception and met him at the bottom.

Harriet Bedell: deaconess, tireless worker, advocate for the poor, and most of all—an ardent follower of Christ.

Let's talk

Harriet spent her whole life as a missionary and teacher, teaching people about Jesus. Who are some of the people in your life who have taught you about Jesus?

Some people thought Harriet couldn't do the things she did because she was a woman. Later in life, people thought she couldn't do her work because she was older. Have you ever done something that people didn't think that you could do? What did that teach you?

Harriet traveled from Alaska to Florida and many places in between, following Jesus on a big adventure. What kind of adventure would you like to go on with Jesus?

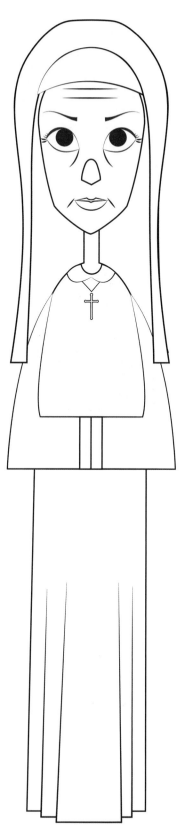

Harriet Bedell

Óscar Romero

Almighty God, you called your servant **Óscar Romero** to be a voice for the voiceless poor, and to give his life as a seed of freedom and a sign of hope: Grant that, inspired by his sacrifice and the example of the martyrs of El Salvador, we may without fear or favor witness to your Word who abides, your Word who is Life, even Jesus Christ our Lord, to whom, with you and the Holy Spirit, be praise and glory now and for ever. **Amen.** (*Lesser Feasts and Fasts,* p. 211)

Tell me a story

Have you ever heard news so good you couldn't help but share it? Have you ever heard something so wonderful that you couldn't keep it to yourself? Have you ever known a story so amazing that you wanted to tell it to everyone, everywhere, all the time?

Born in El Salvador in 1917, Óscar Romero was a shy boy who loved books… and he loved God. At the age of thirteen, he decided he would like to be a priest. He went to Rome where he read and studied many books: the Bible, the lives of the saints, and the writings of the great teachers of the church.

And as he read, Óscar learned some good news. He learned the good news of God, in whose image each one of us is created. He learned the good news of Jesus, who loved us so much he gave his life for us. He learned the good news of the Holy Spirit, who promises to live in our hearts and move in our lives, so that we can serve God in the world. In the Bible, Óscar read the words of Jesus, who said:

> Blessed are the poor in spirit, for theirs is the kingdom of heaven.
> Blessed are those who mourn, for they will be comforted.
> Blessed are the meek, for they will inherit the earth.
> Blessed are those who hunger and thirst for righteousness, for they will be filled.
> Blessed are the merciful, for they will receive mercy.
> Blessed are the pure in heart, for they will see God.
> Blessed are the peacemakers, for they will be called children of God.
> Blessed are those who are persecuted for righteousness' sake, for theirs is the kingdom of heaven.
> (Matthew 5:1-10)

This was good news, great news, the best and most amazing news. It was news so wonderful that Óscar couldn't keep it to himself. He had to tell someone; he had to tell everyone. And so he did.

Óscar Romero became a priest, and then a bishop, and then the archbishop of El Salvador. He traveled all over his country, preaching and teaching the good news of Jesus. Óscar told people that the poor were blessed, and that we needed to help everyone have food and water and homes and safety. Óscar told people that peacemakers are children of God, and we must turn away from all violence and killing. Óscar told people the good news of God's great love in Jesus Christ.

But at that time in El Salvador, where Óscar lived, the government was corrupt. The rich wanted to keep all their riches for themselves; they didn't want to share what they had with the poor. The powerful wanted to keep all the power, so they used violence to scare and kill the people who disagreed with them. The rich and the powerful in El Salvador did not want Óscar to tell people the great good news of God's love for the poor and the lowly.

But Óscar just couldn't keep quiet. He couldn't help but share the amazing news of God's love for all people. Over and over, Oscar preached and taught that all people were made in the image of God, that all people were worthy of love and care, that all people deserved food and shelter and safety.

Óscar begged the soldiers in El Salvador to lay down their weapons. "The peasants you kill are your own brothers and sisters. When you hear the voice of the man commanding you to kill, remember instead the voice of God. Thou Shall Not Kill…In the name of God, in the name of our tormented people whose cries rise up to heaven, I beseech you, I beg you, command you, stop the repression."

Óscar knew that it was dangerous to keep saying these things, to preach what Jesus had taught, to declare God's love to the world. He knew that the government and the soldiers didn't like to hear that they would have to change their behavior. But he also knew that God's love is stronger than anything, even death. So he kept sharing God's great news.

On March 24, 1980, Óscar was celebrating Holy Communion with a group of nuns when he was shot and killed. His assassin was never caught.

Óscar Romero had news that was too good not to share: the great good news of God's love in Jesus Christ. He preached and taught and shared that news no matter what, until the very end of his life. Because of Óscar Romero, many hundreds of people heard and believed the good news of God. They learned that they were created in God's image. They heard that they were loved by Jesus. They believed that they were filled with the Holy Spirit. Eventually, El Salvador found peace —in large part, because Óscar Romero and others like him kept proclaiming the good news of God, no matter what.

Let's talk

How do you think Óscar Romero leaned on God when he felt scared?

Óscar told the truth, even when it was scary or dangerous. Have you ever had to tell the truth when it was scary? What was that like?

What good news about God do you think that people most need to hear?

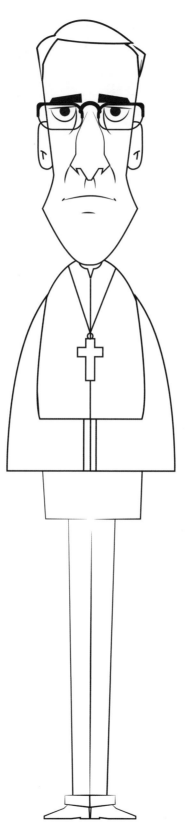

Óscar Romero

resources

Meet the Saints: Family Storybook can be used as part of a Christian formation program, including a component of the youth and adult version of *Living Discipleship: Celebrtating the Saints*. A Facilitator's Guide is available for teachers and leaders at www.forwardmovement.org. Additional resources can be found at www.livingdiscipleship-fm.org.

Picture Book Suggestions
Below is a list of picture books on various saints that can be used along with the curriculum.

Mary, the mother of Jesus
- *Mary* by Brian Wildsmith. Eerdmans Books for Young Readers, 2002.
- *Mary, Mother of Jesus* by Mary Joslin. Loyola Press, 1999.
- *Mary: the Mother of Jesus* by Tomie dePaola. Holiday House, 1995.
- *The Story of Mary, the Mother of God* by Dorrie Papademetriou. St. Vladimirs Seminary Press, 2000.

Patrick and Brigid
- *Patrick: Patron Saint of Ireland* by Tomie dePaola. Holiday House, 1992.
- *Brigid's Cloak* by Bryce Milligan. Eerdmans Books for Young Readers, 2002.
- *The Life of Saint Brigid: Abbess of Kildare* by Jane Meyer. Conciliar Press, 2009.

Hildegard of Bingen
- *Hildegard's Gift* by Megan Hoyt. Paraclete Press, 2014.
- *The Secret World of Hildegard* by Jonah Winter. Arthur A. Levine Books, 2007.

Claire
- *Clare and Francis* by Guido Visconti. Wm. B. Eerdmans Publishing Co., 2003.

Martin Luther
- *Martin Luther: A Man Who Changed the World* by Paul Maier. Concordia Publishing, 2004.
- *Martin Luther: What Should I do?* by Catherine MacKenzie. CF4Kids, 2010.

J.S. Bach
- *Sebastian: A Book about Bach* by Jeanette Winter, HMH Books for Young Readers, 1999.

Martin Luther King Jr.
- *Martin's Big Words: the Life of Dr. Martin Luther King Jr.* by Doreen Rappaport. Hyperion Book CH, 2001.
- *I Have a Dream* by Martin Luther King Jr., illustrated by Kadir Nelson. Schwartz & Wade, 2012.

Below is a list of children's books that explore saints more broadly.

- *Loyola Kids Book of Saints* by Amy Welborn. Loyola Press, 2001.
- *Can you Find Saints?: Introducing Your Child to Holy Men and Women* by Philip D. Gallery. St. Anthony Messenger Press, 2003. Available through Forward Movement.
- *115 Saintly Fun Facts* by Bernadette McCarver Snyder. Liguori Press, 1993.
- *The Church History ABCs: Augustine and 25 Other Heroes of the Faith* by Stephen J. Nichols. Crossway Press, 2010.

about the authors

Melody Wilson Shobe is an Episcopal priest who has served churches in Rhode Island and Texas. A graduate of Tufts University and Virginia Theological Seminary, Melody is currently working on curriculum development for Forward Movement. Melody, her husband, and their two daughters live in Dallas, Texas, where she spends her spare time reading stories, building forts, conquering playgrounds, baking cookies, and exploring nature.

Lindsay Hardin Freeman is a Minnesota-based Episcopal priest, author, and mother. She is the author and/or editor of six books, including the award-winning *Bible Women: All Their Words and Why They Matter* and *The Scarlet Cord: Conversations with God's Chosen Women*. She also has written a children's book, *The Spy on Noah's Ark and Other Bible Stories from the Inside Out*. She is married to Leonard Freeman (a poet, priest, and teacher) and has two sons and four stepchildren.

about Forward Movement

Forward Movement is committed to inspiring disciples and empowering evangelists. While we produce great resources like this storybook, Forward Movement is not a publishing company. We are a ministry.

Our mission is to support you in your spiritual journey, to help you grow as a follower of Jesus Christ. Publishing books, daily reflections, studies for small groups, and online resources is an important way that we live out this ministry. More than a half million people read our daily devotions through *Forward Day by Day,* which is also available in Spanish (*Adelante Día a Día*) and Braille, online, as a podcast, and as an app for your smartphones or tablets. It is mailed to more than fifty countries, and we donate nearly 30,000 copies each quarter to prisons, hospitals, and nursing homes. We actively seek partners across the Church and look for ways to provide resources that inspire and challenge.

A ministry of The Episcopal Church for eighty years, Forward Movement is a nonprofit organization funded by sales of resources and gifts from generous donors. To learn more about Forward Movement and our resources, please visit us at www.forwardmovement.org (or www.adelanteenelcamino.org).

We are delighted to be doing this work and invite your prayers and support.